Wolf Planet

First published 2020 by The Hedgehog Poetry Press

Published in the UK by
The Hedgehog Poetry Press
5, Coppack House
Churchill Avenue
Clevedon
BS21 6QW

www.hedgehogpress.co.uk

ISBN: 978-1-913499-41-9

A CIP Catalogue record for this book is available from the British Library.

Wolf Planet

A Space Age Folktale

by

Oz Hardwick

This chapbook is dedicated to fellow lycanthropes and astronauts.

Wolf Planet

A Space Age Folktale

Ahead of schedule, we're entering the realm of science fiction, strapping ourselves into reclining chairs, watching screens fill with a planet that looks something like the Earth we remember, but less detailed, less hospitable. Entering into the spirit of things, we adopt expressions of heroic concentration and end each sentence with *Over*. Who'd have thought that dystopia would be so mundane? Who'd have thought that parallel worlds would be stacked so tight that there'd be no room left to breathe? Rivers run black, and when we check the likelihood of a breathable atmosphere, the data's inconclusive, winking digits demanding caution while confirming the lack of alternatives. Scans estimate a population of almost eight billion humans, but the only voice in our retro headsets, sizzling through static that blisters like boiling fat, is the Big Bad Wolf, suggesting last minute adjustments and promising a warm, warm welcome.

Sometimes the most important decisions come down to generic tropes and narrative expectations, and I momentarily consider a young girl running through a dark wood, a proud pig thatching his dream home, raising a licked anthropomorphic finger to test the weather; but we're locked into our story like a rebel ship in a tractor beam, braced for a battle against insurmountable odds. We prepare ourselves for impact, exchanging steely smiles as the galaxy howls like a wolf. I wonder at what point I should reach for your hand.

When the world tilts and crashes, the only landmark is the cracked ceiling. We understand certainty in the way it snakes through the history of our desires, a catalogue of the errors that have brought us to this pretty pass. We confess to days in which we acceded willingly to the pull of tidal chemistry, but feel no contrition, expect no absolution. So, when the circle of widescreen ambition and realistic possibilities closes, we look beneath the eyes of our unfamiliar companions, our unfamiliar selves, speak of songs and loss, and hide ourselves further within our suspended needs. It is impossible to deny the dissolution of drugs and bodies, the accumulation of midnights, the invisible scars; but the cracks on the ceiling are shaping themselves into roads and veins that animate our undeniable now.

Streets here are a question of ownership, a question of right or wrong, a question mark hanging like a hot air balloon over a swollen river. I don my protective cynicism and step alone into all our stories, sifting soft accretions of coffee, shared cigarettes, and smuggled wine; stopping at phone boxes to call the only numbers I remember, listening to the speaking clock and hits from the early 70s, leaving messages on answerphones I'll regret in the morning. I lose myself in window displays that haven't changed in decades, with tinned meat and carnival masks fading in the tungsten glow. I find the places where there are still gas lamps and the warm shit from horse-drawn trams and drays; steam-blind pub windows where drunken sailors tick every cliché in the book. I run sticks along wrought iron railings to wake the dead, then shoulder the uncanny weight of suppressed wars as I help the bird-thin ghost of my father to his feet. A steam train whistles in the distance, a telephone rings in an abandoned police station, and the gas jet of a hot air balloon blasts overhead. I look up to see my father again, younger than I ever knew him, waving down, sharp in his summer whites, pointing to a place beyond the map's edge. A cart rattles in a cobbled square, gathering up all the stories I've left behind, while I collect empty bottles for the threepenny deposits. Right or wrong, these streets are mine, and one of these nights I'll buy the whole damn town.

Future and *past* are indistinguishable here, but churches bloom and fade as supermarkets rise and fall. It's a matter of tides and needs, of lies and deeds, of sky and seed: all things flower in the correct angle of light. In the avenues of pound stores and charities, a cortege of shopping trolleys weaves its solemn duty past bowing queues at empty cash machines, leeching respect from doorway smokers and buskers with cheap amplifiers who only know two songs, both sad. Some days we are all priests – regardless of gender, sexuality, or beliefs – and rain is our ministry, dirt our solemn duty. The procession passes, all name tags and grudging smiles, clicking loose change like rosaries. Everything has a sell-by date, and the Saturday girl arranges wilting flowers, lights half-price candles with her unfinished homework. Thy will be done. Have a nice day.

On a bench on a corner, the Big Bad Wolf sits, blowing on rigid fingers bitten from hands that have fed him. It's so cold that he can hide his yellow grin behind his own breath. He hands me a tourist guide that shows nothing but exit roads and the Canis Major Dwarf Galaxy, crosses himself, then crosses the street whistling 'Jesus Wants Me For A Sunbeam,' his rough paw slapping a child's tambourine.

In this light, the church is a circus, with all its barkers and rattly old hymns, its charred ceilings and collection plates. The way these coins sing could raise the remaining dead: the way the grass grows in the

7

turnstile aisles could bury the living. Stained-glass severed heads glance every which way, astonished by bulls and eagles, though they've been here forever. Saints and sinners squirm in the erotics of revelation, and there's no rubric or concordance to point the way out, no divine GPS to lead the faithless to the river. Every god you could name is too busy to take calls, and those old-time pardons and declarations won't keep the baby fed. Way out through a broken lancet, a figure that could be either Jesus or the Pied Piper is walking on the municipal swimming pool, smiling children sinking at his feet, still waiting for the clowns and jugglers, still waiting for the saints to go marching in.

Across the parking lot, there's nothing but sea-blue pawprints on asphalt, and a trail of confetti stars; winter flowers frozen in glass bouquets. In a trailer at the city's edge, children warm their hands at a propane ring, while the North Wind invites itself in and a scabby mutt dreams itself into the Big Bad Wolf. Just as the technology we dreamed of in the 60s has let us down time after time, so our fairy tales are less remarkable in their fruition: goblin tailors sleep beneath their benches, talking donkeys' riddles are nothing but hot air, and even the flophouses have no homes for mermaids as they stagger into an unfamiliar world of legs and gravity. That said, I still feel obliged to collect the spells and glitter that litter the ring road verges, label them in invisible ink, and lay them in an airtight musical box with a ballerina who escapes every full Moon. When no one's looking, the children are bears or pigs, or some other shorthand anthropomorphism; the Big Bad Wolf pours himself a drink and flips through dog-eared cards at a Formica table, and shoes repair themselves one more time before morning. Transformation isn't all it's cracked up to be, and names aren't that hard to guess. There are flowers wilting in abandoned supermarket trolleys, flowers taped with rain-smeared cards to viaduct railings. The flame beneath the cauldron flickers, a needle sits, half piercing a stiff hem, and a grey tail shimmers above the memory of sea.

This, I realise, was my childhood home: footprints of furniture marking some kind of trail; childish knuckleprints in polystyrene tiles; scraps of 50s lino at the bottoms of built-in wardrobes. In the room where I was born, my mother's hair streams beneath the mirror. Beyond a wall that's nothing but sheet music and shopping lists, I lost my virginity: maybe it's still there somewhere among the boxes of cards, photos, and Christmas decorations, but it's too late to look now. Down the hall, my heart was broken more than once: some of the pieces are amongst the ornaments and souvenirs cluttering the cabinet at the top of the stairs. There is an eggshell I blew hollow, and the back bedroom's full of garden gnomes. I leave through a Tupperware airlock, floating like the image on an overexposed Polaroid.

By the time I find you again, you are sleeping in a hall lined with crooning radios, your dreams rising and falling like the North Sea, your coarse sheets rustling like agitated sand. It's a sleep bought with cigarette coupons, chosen from a glossy catalogue then lost for fifty years. Your family is no longer at this address, but the doorbell rings like a calliope, and you swing your smooth brown legs from under a mountain of half-remembered half-truths, and are unbolting the door before you can say *Big Bad Wolf*. Before you know it, there's cocoa in hand-thrown mugs, I'm toasting crumpets on the snickering fire, and the Big Bad Wolf settles himself in the slack-sprung armchair to tell you a story. His voice is a yet another radio lost between stations, a pirate on twenty a day, but you have never felt so safe, and you close your tiny fists into that soft, warm belly fur as he hums you back into yourself.

It's a story of June in the South, all dust and pollen, with straw houses leaning against the weight of the Sun. It's dry dry dry, and every day cracks a little more, with fissures in the tarmac opening into archaeological surprises. Amongst the bones and bottle caps, strap-ends and lead badges speak of faith, feast and famine, fear and fucking; the same old same old that ripples the surface until it almost, nearly, not quite tears. And here comes the Big Bad Wolf again, shimmering out of a high noon blacktop mirage, red-eyed, licking his lips and zipping his fly, weighing his huff and puff against all those generations sleeping, season after season, beneath his scorched paws. He cracks a smile as he whistles hello to those li'l ol' pigs. The Sun is high high high. Atishoo, atishoo, dust to dust. Amen.

It's important to remember that when no one else can hear, wolves sing falsetto, their pitch shifting like moistened fingers on the rims of wineglasses. Wolves, of course, know nothing of glass, sipping wine from silver goblets inscribed with scenes from wolf history and wolf folktale. Wolves can't read, but they forget nothing, retelling their stories time after time, as cleanly as biting into an apple. Wolves have no use for apples, preferring the taste of meat and stories: they have no interest in spices or metaphors, and all their anecdotes end with feasting. When they enter the town, dressed in neutral suits and colourful ties, wolves don't sing at all, keeping their voices for casual greetings and pragmatic alliances; but when they queue for coffee, and when they slump into the backs of taxis, their every nerve howls.

Sleepwalk or spacewalk: everything moves in slow motion here. Ownership is elastic, and books change hands like hands change gloves. Gloved hands finger the nap of fine cloth and riffle notes of varying denominations. What's nominally yours is really mine, and vice versa, and even verse has no definitive attributions. Daily ablutions are all *you wash my back, I'll wash yours*, though there's a shiv and a fifty up every sleeve. No one leaves and there are no strangers, but every night the bunks carry different sleepers. Sleep is elastic here, the dividing line between daily grind and dream stretched thin as a surgical glove. Love snaps back and stings, wolves sing in twisted fairy tale parking lots, and barely a bark distinguishes predator from pet. Poppy petals flip like pages in borrowed and bartered books, like blood on bare hands, expanding precise distinctions to the point of abstraction.

This may or may not be a dream, but flashing signs demand we adapt and survive: reskill, deskill, destress, dress down, dress to impress, dress for success, keep our cards close to our chests, show no weakness, never pause for breath, never even pause for death, because winners never sleep, you win or you weep, fly high or dive deep, sharp eye or slapped cheek, sharp edge or window ledge, all meat and no veg, grab the thick end of the wedge, stab the victor in the back, art for art's sake, heart attack, start-up failures make the man, kick the pricks or kick the can, down in one or down the pan, don't fall for mutton dressed as lamb, be the Big Bad Wolf in the hunt for ham, because you can't be bigger than the big *I am*, so plan to pull the perfect heist, there's no Plan B in Paradise, your parachute is always open, the smartest word is the word unspoken, nothing's fixed if nothing's broken, always sleep with both eyes open, it's an eye for an eye and a shot in the dark, the city streets are no walk in the park, the best defence is always attack, a bird in the hand makes a nutritious snack, the red eye express is a route to the black, if it looks like a duck it'll probably quack, but you can't make an omelette when you're strung-out on crack, and when the barrel's in your mouth there's no turning back.

Stop!

In the dark, our hearts beat so close they could be two sides of the same drum, syncopating with the city's lopsided jazz. On Main Street, wolves wear the sweltering night buttoned tight around their shaggy necks. They've given up on scrub and steppe, headed to where cicadas sing and margaritas come in chilled jugs with sugared rims. All through the day, there's been flesh on display; bums, guns and guts reddening in flip-flopped afternoons, overripe for the tasting, burnt silly with the freedoms of minibreak madness. But the brief nights are best, with the skunk-humming, pre-loaded party animals stagger-swaggering in slurred strobes, pop-eyed blind and limp by the bins. Away in the west, a lighthouse winks and looks away. Wolves loosen their collars, tap ringed fingers on the seafront rail, lick the spittle from their cornered grins as they sniff the sweat and cologne. *What big dreams you have*, but it's 4am and the bass ripples the sea to wake the irritable world, and the wolves are rolling up their sleeves, nodding their heads to the irresistible beat.

On the city's flipside, it's late-night shopping, and the streets are heaving with empty pockets, empty baskets, and empty hearts that only beat through habit. Snow slips out from glitzy window displays, snapping at fingers and turning to slush in old boots. When we try to speak, our tongues are frozen. We have read about days like these, but when we search for those familiar stories, the library is closed, the books turning to icy pulp in rusty skips, their stories bowdlerised and redacted into cosy memes and adverts for mornings that had already sold out when we were children. There are untidy queues at the food bank and A&E, stretching into the New Year like discarded ribbons from a gift no one wanted, crossing and re-crossing in schools and church halls. Even the Moon is slowly hiding her face. But there are embers in each hearth and brazier that can kindle into flame, and promises pouring through each letterbox to feed the fire. Light the candles one by one. Everything will be wrapped up long before midnight, there are no returns, and the future is for life, not just for Christmas.

Towards the dawn, the music creeps up the back stairs, trailing cheap wine and cigarettes, hot under distressed leather. Its hair's mussed up and its boots are scuffed, and it speaks in an accent that could be San Francisco or Shangri-La as it whispers at the keyhole like the Big Bad Wolf himself. It drums on the jamb like forbidden dancing, greased back and sly, pulse-deep and insistent; but when you open the door there's nothing there but the last of the big city night, with all its tired garbage carts and sirens. You listen for rhythms in the distant traffic, in the push and pull of elevators and underground trains, but there's only hushed voices turning you back to sleep. So you close the door like a prayer book but, when you turn, there's the music, sprawled and grinning on the beat-up sofa, tap tap tapping on a body-warm bottle that it raises to its red red lips.

All this time, the person I wanted to be has been sitting in an unremarkable car or a decompression chamber, watching the harvest Moon roll and bob amongst trees and pylons. I have been thinking about all the words I've ever said and all the words I should have said, about foundation myths concerning disgraced nuns, and about the employment rights of the dead. It's been a long, long day, and everything is shifting, the mooring ropes of reason flapping in the simple motion of the turning world. There's been a new spate of UFO sightings, and trust in the democratic process is at an all-time low, but

I can see landing lights approaching and, out on the reassuring road, a lumbering pantechnicon is rolling down the light years, delivering the final perfect constellation.

When I open my laptop all the punctuation has gone and I think of eats shoots and leaves lets eat grandma and lets go clubbing seals Ive always thought the last one was going too far but it still prompts a guilty smile particularly with the Photoshopped cubs on a 70s dance floor *What big eyes youve got* Theres that ol Big Bad Wolf again always coming round with his smiles and flowers and a baseball bat behind his back the size of a deadly cartoon Even when all ambiguity is drained from sentences like a cobras milked venom theres still something uncomfortable something tangibly threatening about the ambient language Its like an orchestra all playing the same tune but with no concept of time or like ballroom dancers in an earthquake With each new word meaning becomes less sure so I slap the side of the screen hard like a 60s television with the picture breaking up until suddenly ,,,,',',',,''',,',',',,',,', allthepunctuationarrivesatoncebuttherearenospaces.

... and the universe expands.

Levitation is a matter of time: how long does it take to stop being a leap, to stop being a plummet? How long must a body lose contact with solid ground? It's a matter of distance: why do astronauts float, rather than levitate, as if the miraculous must be earthbound or, rather, in close proximity? Why is one means of cheating gravity any more remarkable than another? This is not a purely academic concern. Take, for example, a telephone call that wakes you at 4am. It takes a few moments to orient yourself, even though you are in a room you have slept in for years, in a bed you have shared with two long-term partners, a regrettable fling, and a cat that outstayed them all; it takes a few moments longer to recognise your phone's ringtone and to order the many possibilities it carries. When you finally answer it – after maybe twenty seconds or maybe a week – it takes further time before you recognise the accent and characteristic inflections: and you are perplexed by the voice that seeps from the lightweight handset; because although it introduces itself as the police, or a doctor, or a close family member, you know it is gravity, calling from somewhere you think you read about in school but have long since forgotten. And it's here, when all speaking stops, that words hang in the air forever; and if you had children – which in the current circumstances you don't – they would run in and stare, open-mouthed, as if they'd finally caught Father Christmas or the tooth fairy in the act; and they wouldn't notice the glass of water spilled on the carpet, the splashes on the phone, or all your barely recognisable selves circling, adrift from the Earth, certain you'll never come back down.

When I finally return to somewhere I think I recognise, the interchange is an invitation to fade away, to lose myself in the lightning flicker of passing and forgetting. I sink into a stranger's car and listen to their day replaying with all its unreliable signals and stop/start/stop/start familiarities. When they ask me, I tell them I live in the primal forest, with all its Jungian implications and inculcated narratives. They nod in time to the crooner on the radio. By the time they drop me off, I am a ghost in the twisted briars, a prodigal archetype slipped between entries in a library catalogue. Beneath the porchlight, the Big Bad Wolf is waiting for me with a bag full of tinnies and tomorrow's papers, and when we go inside, nothing gives back my reflection.

Who, I ask, first saw animals prowling in the stars: the Great Bear, the Serpent, and our old friend the Big Bad Wolf, snug deep in the southern sky? We dance around such questions, floating in diminished gravity, part-time spacemen bobbing above all surfaces, spinning to Strauss like thrown bones. I ask ol' Wolfie, shaggy sage in his hickory rocker. *Who first saw humans on that untidy planet?* he drawls, licking his trembling lips. *The Butcher, the Baker, the Candlestick Maker? I can't see it myself. Though, if I squint just so –* his left eye snaps shut like a bank vault, his right is a needle's prick in a princess's thumb – *you all look like butchers to me.*

The sun is red, and the air has retreated indoors, waiting until the dust settles. Boxes have been ticked and counted, clear promises have been nailed to the doors of pubs and civic buildings, and the world flutters on in memes and tweets, celebrity spats, football results, and online shopping. On screen, everything looks benign, smug as a Christmas advert, with the smiling poor lining linen-topped tables, eyes bright as tossed coins, eager for the feast that won't arrive, while giggling children unwrap empty boxes for the cameras. Outside, in the barely breathable city, twitchy police finger batons at the first tentative march, and already yesterday's slogans have been filed under dead languages. There are discount codes for empty shops, real-time alerts for cancelled trains, and an app to track every mistake that has led us here. In the ruins of what may once have been a factory or a sports hall, a gramophone plays popular songs from an unreported war, while breathless dancers – eyes closed, bodies hungry and yearning – step intricate patterns in the dust. The mountains call like a pack keening for a stray cub.

Not far from the road, close under the Moon, the path loops and drops. It may be natural, though it's probably an old quarry; but either way it's not a city, and it's as close to nature as we get these days. We didn't plan it, but we're wearing matching scarves, red and threadbare, though yours is tight to your flushed cheeks and mine is loose, blowing like a flag on a fleeing galleon in one of those films they used to show in the school holidays. Any minute we could be ambushed by stop-motion warriors who just keep on coming however hard we press, cutlasses still twitching in their severed limbs. Or maybe a tentacle will rise from the still pool far below, flailing moderately convincing models of ourselves against a bluescreen sky as we wait around and mug for the close-ups. As we cut to the real world, I feel there should be goats in a landscape like this, or at least birds. Aren't there birds everywhere? The wind cuts between slate cliffs, and as one we wrap our scarves around our faces like protesters in Downing Street on the eve of the holidays. Any minute we could be ambushed by police who just keep on coming however peacefully we resist, batons twitching in angry fists. Or maybe a white elephant – say, a water cannon – will hose us off our feet, as moderately convincing news reports frame *troublemakers* and give assurances of reasonable response. As I reach for your hand, I feel there are watchers in every shadow, or at least cameras. Aren't there cameras everywhere? Even through strata of wool and polyester, I can feel your warm skin, as close to nature as we get these days. The path loops and drops. We didn't plan it, but our lips are red as the sky.

A whistle slices through the stillness. In the aftermath of change, nothing changes: the same people with the same dogs, the same gullies where rainwater gathers, the same curtains at the same windows. There are wreaths on doors, bottles in the gutter, and all alarms and sirens are silenced. It's like waking up in hospital with a throat raw from bile and plastic, observed by weary eyes in which concern vies with irritation as each emotion sinks beneath the boredom of life-and-

17

death decisions. I check my pulse as if it belongs to someone else, write down a sequence of digits I don't understand and will lose later on. It's like swallowing the consecrated Host and discovering it's just stale bread, and that it makes no difference to your aching belly, much less your soul, whatever that may be. In the aftermath of change, I pull on the same shirt I wore yesterday, answer incoming messages as if I was drowning and had been thrown an anchor, and take the usual medication. The morning news announces victories and defeats, shows a flag waving in an endless desert, but collateral damage will take time to come to light. A whistle slices through the stillness, and a dog barks.

When all's said and done, the Big Bad Wolf's not so big or bad, so I invite him round for tea every once in a while. We've little in common but long years of huffing and puffing, and it's best to avoid politics or religion with wolves, so we keep conversation insubstantial: how my job's going, what's new in the dark wood, and how there's a trend towards personal redemption and a wider morality in current comedy shows. I reckon this latter's a good thing, but the Big Bad Wolf feigns ambivalence, adhering to his culturally prescribed role. He never stays late, getting twitchy when the light fades and the howling starts, gathering darkness into a concert of freedom and need. When he takes his leave, his paw is hot and wet in my cold hand, and even as we exchange commonplaces on the threshold, I can see his eyes are elsewhere, unpicking the hunger we share but never mention in the spiced heart of my gingerbread house.

So here we are, still braced for touchdown, still spinning at a thousand miles per hour, still blinking in the beauty of astronomical disasters. Gaseous clouds become nothing but light and distance. Crab and Horse Head. Cliffs fall away into the sea and a lighthouse performs its dervish dance, curling back over the horizon. The speed of erosion is relative. Bright points delineate neither archer nor goat, yet everything is connected in a manner impossible to understand. Science, religion, superstition: we choose our metaphors according to momentary contingency. Cliffs fall away into the sea and the Great Wolf snaps at the Moon. Eagle. Seven Sisters. Beauty of shift and reception. Bright points delineate neither hunter nor dog. Out on the waves, a shadow of a boat. Arbitrary intersections of perception and belief. A meditation of lighthouses. Blink. Light and distance.